KINGFISHER
LONDON & NEW YORK

This selection copyright © 2007 by Macmillan Publishers
International Ltd
Illustrations copyright © 2004, 2005, 2006, 2007 by Martin
Chatterton and 2004, 2005 by Tony Trimmer
Cover illustration copyright © 2007 by Martin Chatterton

Some material in this edition was previously published in the
following volumes: *Boo!*, *Ho, Ho, Ho!*, *Seriously Silly School Jokes*,
Yuck! The Grossest Joke Book Ever!, and *What a Hoot!*

Published in the United States by Kingfisher,
175 Fifth Ave., New York, NY 10010
Kingfisher is an imprint of Macmillan Children's Books, London.
All rights reserved.

Distributed in the U.S. and Canada by Macmillan, 175 Fifth Ave.,
New York, NY 10010

Library of Congress Cataloging-in-Publication Data
Chatterton, Martin.
Sidesplitters: a joke a day: 365 guaranteed giggles/illustrated by
Martin Chatterton & Tony Trimmer
p. cm.
ISBN 978-0-7534-6128-0
1. Juvenile wit and humor. I. Trimmer, Tony. II. Title.
PN6166.C43 2007
818'.5402—dc22   2007045649

ISBN: 978-0-7534-6128-0

Kingfisher books are available for special promotions and
premiums. For details contact: Special Markets Department,
Macmillan, 175 Fifth Ave., New York, NY 10010.

For more information, please visit www.kingfisherbooks.com

Printed in the UK by CPI Mackays, Chatham ME5 8TD

8 10 9 7

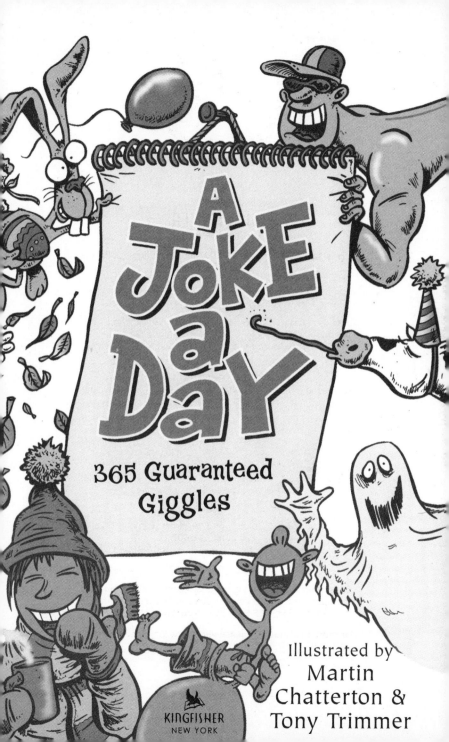

A JOKE a DAY

365 Guaranteed Giggles

Illustrated by
**Martin Chatterton &
Tony Trimmer**

KINGFISHER
NEW YORK

January

January 1

What's a cow's favorite holiday?
Moo Year's Eve!

January 2

Why do bees hum?
Because they don't know the words.

January 3

What do you get if you cross a skunk with a dinosaur?
A Stinkasaurus.

Spaghetti Day

Customer: Excuse me, waiter, is there spaghetti on the menu?
Waiter: No, madam, I wiped it off.

What's a polygon?
A dead parrot.

Epiphany

Who works in a department store selling perfume?
Frank Incense.

  **Why do cows have bells?** *Because their horns don't work.*

 **What did the mummy say to the detective?** *"Let's wrap up this case."*

What's yellow, brown, and hairy? *A grilled cheese sandwich dropped on the carpet.*

 **January 10**

Why is it difficult to hold a conversation with a goat?
It always butts in.

 **January 11**

What smells, runs all day, and lies around at night with its tongue hanging out?
A pair of old sneakers.

Why did the chicken cross the clothes store?
To get to the other size.

"You're late," said one frog to the other. "I know," he replied. "I got stuck in someone's throat."

What kind of bird can write?
A pen-guin.

January 15

What do dogs call parking meters?
Pay toilets!

January 16

What goes trot-dash-trot-dash-dash?
Horse code.

January 17

What do you get when you cross a cat with a vacuum cleaner?
I don't know, but it drinks a lot of milk!

What did the horse say when he reached the end of his feedbag?
"That's the last straw."

What do you call a fairy that hasn't bathed?
Stinkerbell.

What do you get if you walk under a cow?
A pat on the head.

January
21

How can you catch a squirrel?
Climb up a tree and act like a nut.

January
22

A duck went into a pharmacy and asked for some ointment. "Certainly," said the pharmacist. "Should I put it on your bill?"

January
23

What did the mother buffalo say to her son before he left?
"Bison."

What's worse than taking a bite of your apple and seeing a worm?
Seeing half a worm.

What do you get from a well-educated oyster?
Pearls of wisdom.

Australia Day

What do you call a lazy kangaroo?
A pouch potato.

January 27

What vegetable
can you find in
a toilet?
A leek.

January 28

How can you tell if an elephant
is getting ready to charge?
He pulls out his credit card.

January 29

What do you get if
you put a young goat
in a blender?
A crazy, mixed-up kid.

What does a bat sing in the rain?
"Raindrops Keep Falling on my Feet."

What did the first cannibal say to the second cannibal after they had eaten a clown?
"Is it me, or did that taste a little bit funny?"

February

Why did the boy go to bed early?
Because he was feeling Febru-weary.

What happened when the groundhog met the dogcatcher?
It became a poundhog!

What do you call a fly with no wings?
A walk.

What fairy tale do ghosts like best?
Sleeping Boo-ty.

Why does Batman wear his underwear outside of his pants?
To keep them clean.

What do you give a seasick elephant?
A lot of room.

February 7

What did the biker have written on his leather jacket?

"If you can read this, my girlfriend has fallen off!"

February 8

Kite Flying Day

"Doctor, doctor, I've got so much wind. Do you have anything for it?"

"Yes, here's a kite. Now go and fly it."

Why do seagulls live near the sea?
Because if they lived near the bay, they'd be called bagels.

What do you call a frog with no hind legs?
Unhoppy!

How can you double your money?
By folding it in half.

Lincoln's Birthday

Johnny: Dad, today is Lincoln's Birthday. He was a great man, wasn't he?

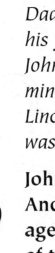

Dad, always eager to teach his young son a lesson: Yes, Johnny, indeed he was. And mind you, when Abraham Lincoln was your age, he was out splitting rails.

Johnny: Yes, Dad, I know. And when he was your age, he was the president of the United States.

What's red, sweet, and bites people?
A jampire.

What happens when you fall in love with a chef?
You get buttered up.

What's a dirty book?
One that's been dropped in the toilet.

Why do witches fly on broomsticks?
Vacuum cleaner cords aren't long enough.

What do you get if you cross a turkey with a banjo?
A bird that plucks itself.

Teacher: Give me three collective nouns.
Student: Wastepaper basket, vacuum cleaner, and dustpan.

What did it say on the door of the pharaoh's tomb?
"Toot 'n' come in."

What do you get if you cross a dog with a telephone?
A golden receiver.

What's gray and has big ears and a trunk?
A mouse going on vacation.

Where did George Washington buy his hatchet?
At the chopping mall.

Where can elephants be found?
Don't be silly—they're much too big to lose.

Why did the porcupine cross the road?
To show that he had guts.

What do you get if you drop a piano down a mine shaft?
A flat minor.

What stands in the middle of Paris?
The letter "r."

What type of streets do zombies like best?
Dead ends.

Why do doctors and nurses wear masks?
So if they make a mistake, the patient won't know who did it!

(Leap years only)

What years do frogs like best?
Leap years.

March

March

1

Pig Day

What do you call a pig that does karate?
A pork chop.

March

2

What books do owls read?
Hoot-dunits.

March

3

What type of tree is good at math?
A geometry.

What is black and white and red all over?
A nun in a blender.

Why did the dinosaur cross the road?
Because the chicken hadn't been invented yet.

Dentist's Day

What did the dentist of the year get?
A little plaque.

March
7

Why did the boy bring toilet paper to the party?
Because he was a party pooper.

March
8

Why do birds fly south in the winter?
Because it's too far to walk.

March
9

What do you call a man with no legs?
Neil.

March
10

What farm animal talks too much?
Blah-Blah Black Sheep.

March
11

How can you tell which spiders are the trendiest?
They have their own websites.

March
12

Why did the boy take his car to school?
To drive his teacher up the wall.

  Which bird is always out of breath?
A puffin.

 What goes "quick, quick"?
A duck with the hiccups.

 What happened when the witch misbehaved at school?
She was ex-spelled.

March
16

What's the most important thing to remember in a chemistry lesson?
Don't lick the spoon.

March
17

St. Patrick's Day

What is Irish and on the lawn all summer?
Paddy O'Furniture.

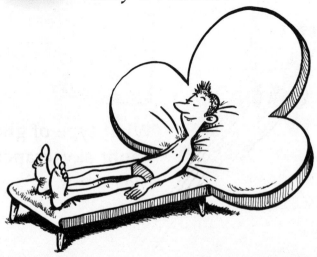

March
18

What do you call a cow with no feet? *Ground beef.*

March
19

What's big and gray and has body odor problems? *A smellyphant.*

March
20

What type of ghosts haunt skyscrapers? *High spirits.*

March 21

What happened to the two bedbugs that fell in love?
They got married in the spring.

March 22

International Goof-off Day

Teacher: Gavin, don't hum while you're working.
Gavin: I'm not working—I'm just humming.

March
23

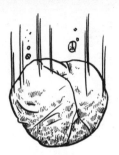

Why is a bunny the luckiest animal in the world?
It has four rabbit's feet.

March
24

How do hedgehogs play leapfrog?
Very carefully.

March
25

Who invented fractions?
Henry the Eighth.

Why were the naughty eggs punished?
Because they kept playing practical yolks.

What do you get if you cross the Atlantic with the *Titanic*?
Halfway.

What happened to the boy who drank eight cans of Coke?
He brought 7Up.

March 29

What do you call a lost monster?

A where-wolf.

March 30

<u>Doctor's Day</u>

"Doctor, Doctor, I feel like a pack of cards."

"I'll deal with you later."

March 31

Why shouldn't you tell an egg a good joke?

It might crack up.

April

April
1

April Fool's Day

Why is everyone tired on April first?
Because they've just finished a 31-day March!

April
2

When do monkeys fall from the sky?
During Ape-ril showers.

Why do polar bears have fur coats?
They don't look good in tweed ones.

What do you get if you pour hot water down a rabbit hole?
Hot cross buns.

Why did the teacher turn on the lights?
Because her students were so dim.

$1 + 1 = 11$

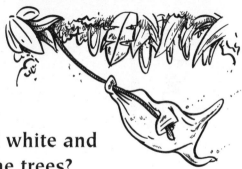

What's green and white and swings through the trees?
Tarzan's handkerchief!

What do you get if you cross an elephant with a sparrow?
Broken telephone wires.

What type of jewelry do rabbits wear?
14–carrot gold.

"**Mommy, mommy, all the kids call me a werewolf!**"
"*Never mind, dear, now go and comb your face.*"

Teacher: **If you had five candy bars and your little brother asked you for one, how many would you have left?**
Student: Five, of course.

What happened when the dog went to the flea circus?
He stole the show.

How do chickens
stay in shape?
They eggsercise.

What do you call a
bear with no ears?
A b.

What do you call a
fish with no eyes?
A fsh.

Teacher: Can anyone tell me the name of the Dog Star?
Pupil: Lassie?

How do witches keep their hair in place while flying?
With scare spray.

What's brown and sounds like a bell?
Dung.

April 18

Why did the boy take a ladder to school?
Because it was a high school.

April 19

What season is it when you are on a trampoline?
Spring.

How many rotten eggs were in the omelet?
A phew.

Where did the vampire keep his valuables?
In a blood bank.

Earth Day

How can you tell if a tree is a dogwood?
By its bark!

April
23

What do you call a
naughty monkey?
A bad-boon.

April
24

Why was the
bunny so upset?
*He was having a
bad hare day.*

What do you call a boomerang that won't come back?
A stick.

Why was the boy sitting in the gerbils' cage?
Because he wanted to be the teacher's pet.

What tools are used in arithmetic?
Multipliers.

April 28

What is a skeleton's favorite musical instrument?
A trombone.

April 29

International Dance Day

Why are dogs such bad dancers?
They have two left feet.

April 30

What's the worst thing you'll find in a school cafeteria?
The food.

May

May 1

Save the Rhino Day

Why do rhinos have so many wrinkles?
Because they are hard to iron.

May 2

Why did the cell cross the microscope?
To get to the other slide.

May 3

Why did the demon undertaker chop up the corpses?
He wanted them to rest in pieces.

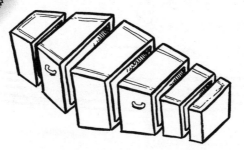

May 4

Respect for Chickens Day

What do you call a chicken that crosses the road, rolls around in the mud, and then comes back?
A dirty double-crosser.

May 5

Cinco de Mayo

What type of cans are there in Mexico?
Mexicans!

No Homework Day

Teacher: How do you like doing your homework?
Student: I like doing nothing better!

What do you get if you cross an elephant and a parakeet?
A very messy cage.

What game do cannibals play?
Swallow the leader.

What's worse than a giraffe with a sore throat?

A centipede with athlete's foot.

What do dogs increase?

The pup-ulation.

What did the daddy ghost say to his family while he was driving?

"Fasten your sheet belts."

May 12

What should you do if you give an elephant chili?
Get out of the way.

May 13

What's green with red spots?
A frog with the chickenpox.

May 14

What do you put
on a pig's pimple?
Oinkment.

May 15

What do they teach
at witch school?
Spelling.

May 16

Why aren't leopards good
at playing hide-and-seek?
They're always spotted.

May
17

Why did knights in armor practice a lot?
To stop them from getting rusty.

May
18

How do ghosts like their eggs cooked?
Terrifried!

May 19

What's a vampire's favorite dance?
The fangdango.

May 20

What do you call the small rivers that run into the Nile?
Juveniles.

Why did the porcupine squeal "Ouch, ouch, ouch!"?
Because he put on his coat inside out.

What goes, "Cluck, cluck . . . BANG"?
A chicken in a minefield.

May
23

<u>World Turtle Day</u>

What did the snail
say when he rode
on the turtle's back?
"Wheeee!"

May
24

Why don't
mummies go
on vacation?
*They're afraid
that they'll relax
and unwind.*

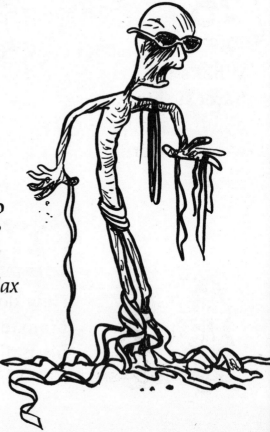

What type of food do math teachers eat?
Square meals.

May 25

May 26

What's the hardest thing about learning to ride a horse?
The ground.

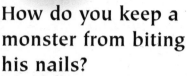

May 27

How do you keep a monster from biting his nails?
Give him some screws.

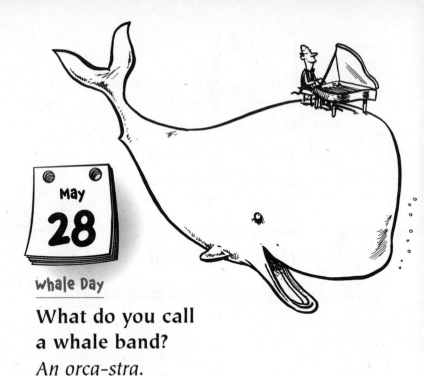

May 28

whale Day

What do you call a whale band?
An orca-stra.

May 29

Mother: Eat your greens; they're good for your skin.
Boy: But I don't want green skin!

Yuck!

May 30

What happened to the glowworm when he was squashed?
He was de-lighted.

May 31

What do you call a monster with no neck?
The Lost Neck Monster.

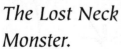

June

How do you get rid of termites?
Exterminite them.

What do lions call antelopes?
Fast food.

What do you call a sleeping bull?
A bulldozer.

Why are cavemen similar to teenagers?
They like to go clubbing.

"Mommy, mommy, the other kids keep calling me a big head."
"Don't worry, darling, there's nothing in it."

Do you want to hear the joke about the pencil?
No. It's pointless.

What do you get if you cross a rabbit with a shallot?
A bunnion.

What day do fish hate?
Fry day.

JuNe
9

How do you stop
a dog from being
sick in the back of a car?
Put it on the front seat.

JuNe
10

What do you get if
you cross a dinosaur
with a wizard?
Tyrannosaurus hex.

JUNE 11

How do you make a milk shake?
Sneak up behind a glass of milk and yell, "Boo!"

JUNE 12

Why doesn't anyone like Dracula?
He has a bat temper.

JUNE 13

Why don't hippos ride bicycles?
The helmets don't fit them.

JUNE 14

What do patriotic monkeys wave on Flag Day?
Star-spangled bananas!

JUNE 15

What game do cows play at parties?
Moosical chairs.

June
16

Why were ancient Egyptian children confused?
Because their daddies were mummies.

June
17

world Juggling Day

How do you kill a circus?
You go for the juggler.

June 18

Have you heard about the good-weather witch? *She's forecasting sunny spells.*

June 19

Butterfly Day

Why couldn't the butterfly go to the dance? *It was a moth ball.*

June 20

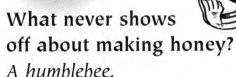

What never shows off about making honey?

A humblebee.

June 21

Who was the most famous French skeleton?

Napoleon Bone-apart.

June 22

What do you get when you run over a parakeet with a lawn mower?

Shredded tweet.

June 23

Who lost a herd of elephants?
Big Bo Peep.

June 24

What's the difference between a toilet brush and a cookie?
You can't dip a toilet brush in your coffee.

June 25

What goes, "Ha-ha-ha—thud"?
A monster laughing his head off.

June 26

Why are giraffes so slow to apologize?
It takes them a long time to swallow their pride.

What do demons have for breakfast?
Deviled eggs.

What's the difference between an Indian elephant and an African elephant?
Around 3,000 miles.

INDIA 1500

AFRICA 1500

June 29

What's the best thing about school?
Vacations.

BBBRRiiiNNG!!

June 30

What's a crocodile's favorite card game?
Snap.

July

Canada Day

What did the beaver say to the tree?
"It's been nice gnawing you."

July 2

What is a vampire's favorite ice cream flavor?
Veinilla.

July 3

Father: Didn't you hear me calling you?
Son: Yes, but you told me not to answer back.

What do you call a patriotic dog?
A Yankee poodle.

What do you call a dirty Teletubby?
Stinky Winky.

What do you call a cat eating a lemon?
A sourpuss.

What does the queen of England do if she burps?
She issues a royal pardon.

Why did the lion lose at poker?
Because he was playing with a cheetah.

July
9

How do you identify
a bald eagle?
*All of his feathers are
combed over to one side.*

July
10

Teddy Bear's Picnic Day

What did the teddy bear say
when he was offered dessert?
"No, thanks, I'm stuffed."

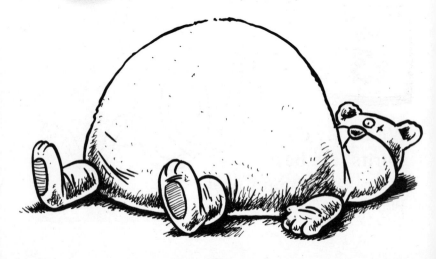

What do you get if you cross a dog with a skunk?
Rid of the dog.

Who exploded at Waterloo?
Napoleon Blown-apart.

What ride do spirits like best at an amusement park?
The roller ghoster.

Bastille Day

Why can't executioners learn French?
Because they know no merci.

Cow Appreciation Day

Where do cows go on vacation?
Moo York.

What is Dracula's favorite fruit?
A neck-tarine.

July
17

How do you get
milk from a cat?
Steal her saucer.

July
18

What do you get if you
cross a dog and a frog?
A croaker spaniel.

July
19

What type of fish do
you find in a birdcage?
A perch.

Why was the stable boy so busy?
Because his work kept piling up.

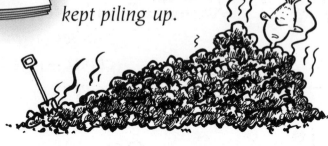

July **21**

How do you make a witch scratch?
Just take away the "w."

July **22**

Why can't you hear a pterodactyl go to the bathroom?
Because it has a silent "p."

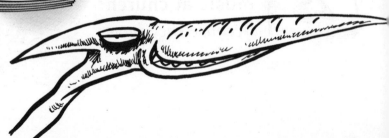

Boy: I thought we had a choice for dinner, but there's only salad.
Mother: That's the choice—take it or leave it!

If you were in the mid-Atlantic facing south, what would be on your right hand?
Four fingers and a thumb.

Why can't skeletons play music at church?
Because they have no organs.

Did you hear about the stupid dog that laid down to eat a bone? *When he stood up, he only had three legs.*

How many insects are needed to fill an apartment building? *Ten ants.*

Hamburger Day

Why did the hamburger go to the gym? *To get better buns.*

How do sheep celebrate their birthdays?
By singing "Happy Birthday to Ewe"!

What do you call a dead cow that's come back to life?
Zombeef.

Why did the cannibal join the police force?
So that he could grill his suspects.

August

August
1

How can you tell the difference between canned beans and canned tuna?
Read the labels.

August
2

What happened to the dog who ate garlic?
His bark was worse than his bite.

August
3

"Doctor, doctor, do the tests show that I'm normal?"
"Yes, yes, both your heads are fine."

What has antlers and sucks blood?
A moose-quito.

What's the difference between Brussels sprouts and a booger?
You can't get a kid to eat Brussels sprouts.

Where can you buy a chess set?
At a pawnshop.

August 7

What kind of bears like bad weather?
Drizzly bears.

August 8

What type of music does a ghost like?
Anything he can boo-gie to.

August 9

What happened to the shark who swallowed a bunch of keys?
He got lockjaw.

August 10

Why didn't the angry witch ride her broom?
She was afraid of flying off the handle.

August
11

What's so great about a neurotic doll?
It comes already wound up.

August
12

What is green and sings?
Elvis Parsley.

August
13

What do you get if you eat baked beans and onions?
Tear gas.

August 14

What do you get if you cross a toad with a galaxy?
Star warts.

August 15

Why did the vampire subscribe to *The Wall Street Journal*?
He heard it had a great circulation.

August 16

What's the best thing to put into a turkey dinner?
Your teeth!

Sandcastle Day

What do you call a witch who lives at the beach?
A sand-witch.

"Waiter, waiter, there's a hand in my soup?"
"That's not your soup, sir; that's a finger bowl."

August 19

What happens when two snails have a fight?
They slug it out.

August 20

What did the Japanese tourist wear in Alaska?
An Eskimono.

August 21

What happened to the guy who didn't pay his exorcist?
He was re-possessed.

August 22

Be an Angel Day

What did one angel say to the other angel?
"Halo there!"

Why did the flea lose his job?
Because he wasn't up to scratch.

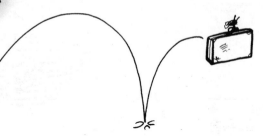

Mother: I know you're disappointed with your birthday present, Billy, but remember—it's the thought that counts.
Billy: Couldn't you have thought a little bigger?

August 25

What's a monster's favorite bean?
A human bean.

August 26

Toilet Paper Day

Why did the toilet paper roll down the hill?
It wanted to get to the bottom.

August 27

What's black and white and eats like a horse?
A zebra.

August 28

What do you give a sick snake?
Asp-irin.

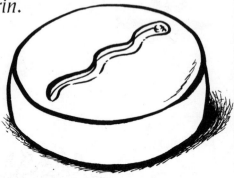

August 29

What's the best time to buy a parakeet?
When they're going cheep.

What does a skeleton order at a restaurant?
Spareribs.

What did the judge say to the skunk?
"Odor in the courtroom!"

September

September
1

What's gray and goes around and around?
An elephant in a washing machine.

September
2

What do ghosts have for dessert?
Booberry ice scream.

September
3

What did the frog say at the dinner party?
"Time's fun when you're having flies."

What do you call a stupid skeleton?
A bonehead.

Be Late for Something Day

Teacher: Why are you always late for school?
Student: Because you keep ringing the bell before I get here.

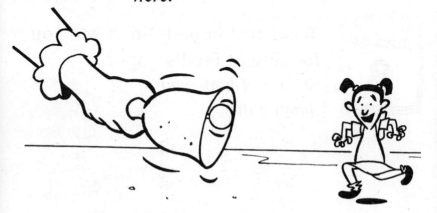

September 6

Why was the principal worried?
Because there were so many rulers at the school.

September 7

Why are fish so smart?
Because they live in schools.

September 8

Teacher: I hope I didn't see you looking at Fred's paper.
Student: I hope you didn't either.

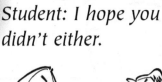

Why do dogs run in circles?
It's hard to run in pentagons.

Teacher: Can anyone name a liquid that won't freeze?
Student: Hot water?

September 11

Why did the teacher wear sunglasses?
Because her pupils were so bright.

September 12

What has four wheels, gives milk, and eats grass?
A cow on a skateboard.

September 13

International Chocolate Day

What did the boy say to his chocolate bar?
"Nice to melt you."

September
14

What do snakes like to study at school?
Hisssssstory.

September
15

What do you call two people who embarrass you at Open House?
Mom and Dad.

No!

September 16

(Tunday, Tonday, Triday, Tednesday)

Teacher: Name two days of the week that begin with "t."

Student: Today and tomorrow.

September 17

What's the difference between school lunches and dog food?

School lunches come on plates.

September 18

What type of jewelry do witches wear?

Charm bracelets.

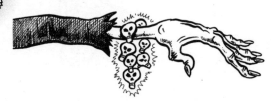

What did one pirate say to the other pirate?
"How AAARRRGGGGHHHHH you doing?"

Why don't skeletons ever go out on the town?
Because they don't have any body to go out with.

September 21

How do you know that it's raining cats and dogs?
You step in a poodle.

September 22

Teacher: Write the longest sentence you can.
Student: Easy! "Life imprisonment."

Why did the secretary have all of her fingers chopped off?

Because she wanted to do shorthand.

Punctuation Day

How can you tell a cat from a comma?

A cat has claws at the end of its paws, and a comma's a pause at the end of a clause.

Why do giraffes have long necks?
Because their feet smell.

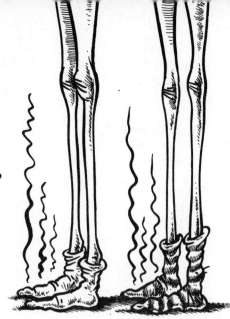

What is a vampire's favorite sport?
Casketball.

September
27

What type of shoes do frogs wear?
Open-toad.

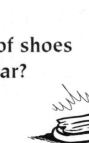

September
28

What is Beethoven doing in his grave?
Decomposing.

September
29

What do you do
when a pig has a
heart attack?
Call a hambulance!

November
26

"Waiter, waiter, there's
a fly in my soup!"
*"Well, throw it a pea, and
it can play water polo."*

October

October 1

What is a baby ghost's favorite game?

PeekaBOO!

October 2

Why didn't the skeleton cross the road?

Because he didn't have the guts.

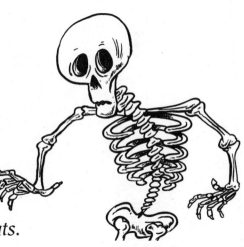

October 3

What type of dog do vampires like best?

Bloodhounds.

October
4

Why do mummies have trouble keeping friends?
They're too wrapped up in themselves.

October
5

What do you call someone who keeps on talking even when no one is listening?
A teacher.

October
6

What's big and green and goes, "Oink, oink"?
Frankenswine.

October
7

Why was the witch kicked out of school?
Because she failed spelling.

October
8

Who was the famous skeleton detective?
Sherlock Bones.

October
9

Why wasn't the vampire working?
He was taking a coffin break.

October
10

Ghost: Where do fleas go in the winter?
Werewolf: Search me!

October
11

What is a mummy's favorite type of music?
Wrap!

October 12

Why did the one-eyed monster have to close his school?

Because he only had one pupil.

October 13

What type of pets do ghosts have?

Scaredy-cats.

October 14

Why does Dracula take art classes?

He likes to draw blood.

Why are skeletons so calm?
Because nothing gets under their skin.

What type of music do witches play?
Hagtime.

Why do vampires need mouthwash?
Because they have bat breath.

Why are pixies such messy eaters?
Because they are always goblin their food.

Why did the headless horseman go into business?
Because he wanted to get ahead in life.

What do you call a wizard from outer space?
A flying sorcerer.

How do monsters predict the future?
They read their horrorscope.

Why isn't Dracula invited to many parties?
Because he's a pain in the neck.

Where do ghosts go swimming?
The Dead Sea.

October 24

What do you call two witches who live together?
Broommates.

October 25

What trees do ghouls like best?
Ceme-trees!

October 26

What do you call a prehistoric ghost?
A terror-dactyl.

Why did the vampire go to the orthodontist?
To improve his bite.

Why did the ghost starch her sheets?
So that she could scare everyone stiff.

What do skeletons say before eating?
"Bone Appetit!"

October 30

What do you get if you cross a witch with an iceberg?
Cold spells.

October 31

Halloween

What do you do when 50 zombies surround your house?
Hope it's Halloween!

November

What type of music do ghosts like?
Spirituals.

What did the slug say as he fell off a branch?
"How slime flies."

Man: Can I have a parrot for my son, please?
Pet store owner: Sorry, sir, we don't do exchanges here.

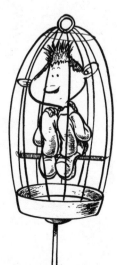

November 4

What did the donkey that only had weeds to eat say?

"Thistle have to do."

November 5

What do you get when you cross a dinosaur with fireworks?

Dinomite.

November 6

Why did Dracula visit the doctor?
Because of his coffin.

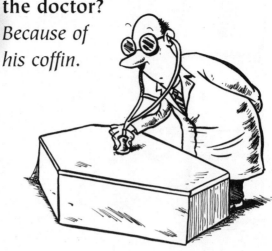

November 7

Why did the owl say, "Tweet, tweet"?
Because she didn't give a hoot.

November 8

Boy snake: Dad, are we poisonous?
Dad snake: Yes, son, why do you ask?
Boy snake: I've just bitten my tongue.

November 9

What do you get when you cross a penguin and an alligator?
I don't know, but don't try to fix its bow tie.

November
10

Why did the fly fly?
Because the spider spied her.

November
11

Why is it difficult to keep a secret when you're cold?
Because your teeth chatter.

November
12

What do you call a sheep with no legs or head?
A cloud.

BAA!

What does a nearsighted gingerbread man use for eyes?
Contact raisins.

Why can't two elephants go swimming at the same time?
Because they only have one pair of trunks.

November 15

Why won't banks allow kangaroos to open accounts?
Their checks always bounce.

November 16

What do you give a sick canary?
Tweetment.

November 17

Why did the skeleton stay up late studying?
Because he was boning up for his exams.

November 18

What did the bald man say when he got a comb for his birthday?

"Thanks, I'll never part with it."

November 19

How can you identify a math plant?

It has square roots.

November
20

Where's the best
place to have the
school nurse's
office?
*Next to the
cafeteria.*

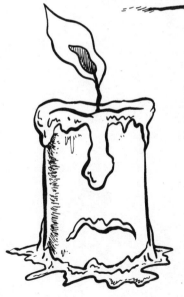

November
21

What was the cold,
evil candle called?
*The Wicked Wick of
the North.*

November 22

What makes the turkey such a fashionable bird?
He's always well dressed for dinner.

November 23

What bird has wings but cannot fly?
A roast turkey.

November 24

Who is never hungry at Thanksgiving?
The turkey—he's always stuffed!

What do vampires put on their turkey?
Grave-y.

This turkey tastes like an old sofa?
Well, you asked for something with plenty of stuffing.

November 27

Why did they let the turkey join the band?
Because it had the drumsticks.

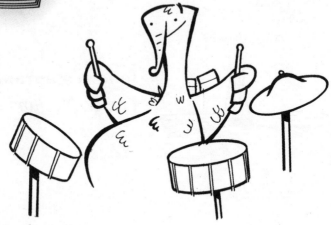

November 28

Where do ponies go when they're sick?
The horse-pital.

November
29

What did the frog order at the fast-food restaurant?
French flies and a diet croak.

November
30

Teacher: Who can tell me what the Scots mean by "lads and lasses"?
Student: I know! Lads are boys, and lassies are dogs.

December

What do you have in December that you don't have in any other month?
The letter "d."

How does Rudolf know when Christmas is coming?
He looks at his calen-deer.

What is green, covered with tinsel, and says, "Ribbet, ribbet"?
A mistle-toad.

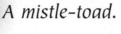

December 4

Who brings
Christmas presents
to baby sharks?
Santa Jaws.

December 5

How do Chihuahuas
say "Merry Christmas"?
"Fleas Navidog"!

December 6

Why do mummies
like Christmas
so much?
*Because of all
of the wrapping!*

December 7

What's red, white, and blue at Christmastime? *A sad candy cane.*

December 8

"Doctor, doctor, help! I've swallowed some Christmas decorations."

"Yes, I can see that you have a touch of tinselitis."

December
9

What do you get if you cross an apple with a Christmas tree?

A pineapple!

December
10

What do you call a chicken at the North Pole?

Lost.

December 11

Why did the gingerbread man go to the doctor?
Because he was feeling crummy!

December 12

What do you get if you cross an Irish setter and a pointer at Christmastime?
A pointsetter.

December 13

What happens when Frosty the Snowman gets dandruff?
He gets snowflakes.

December 14

What do reindeer always say before telling you a joke?
"This one will sleigh you!"

December 15

Why did the elf sleep in the fireplace?
Because he wanted to sleep like a log.

December 16

What's red and white and red and white and red and white?
Santa Claus rolling down a hill.

December 17

How did Rudolf learn to read?
He was elf-taught.

December 18

What do they call a wild elf in Texas?
Gnome on the range!

December 19

What is Santa's favorite cereal?
Frosted flakes.

December 20

What Christmas carol is popular in the desert?
"O Camel Ye Faithful."

December 21

What type of pine has the sharpest needles?

A porcupine.

December 22

What did the sheep say to the shepherd?

"Season's Bleatings!"

December 23

What do you get if you deep-fry Santa Claus?

Crisp Cringle.

Christmas Eve

Why does Santa go down the chimney on Christmas Eve?

Because it soots him.

Christmas Day

What does Santa get if he's stuck in a chimney?

Claustrophobic!

Where does Santa stay when he's on vacation?
At a ho-ho-hotel!

Where did the mistletoe go to become rich and famous?
Hollywood.

What does Frosty the Snowman take when he gets sick?
A chill pill.

What do you get if you cross a skunk with a bell?
Jingle smells.